Reading Comprehension Workbook

Level 5

Series Designer
Philip J. Solimene

Editor
Dorothy M. Bogart

Reading Consultant
Sidney J. Rauch, Ed.D.
Professor of Reading and Education
Hofstra University, New York

EDCON

Story Authors
Sandra Fenichel Asher
Shirley Bogart
Walter Holden
Dorothy Kroll
Ronnie L. Schindel
Malvina Vogel

Copyright © 1997
A/V Concepts Corp.
30 Montauk Blvd, Oakdale NY 11769
info@edconpublishing.com
1-888-553-3266

Visit our Web site at: www.edconpublishing.com

Printed in U.S.A.
ISBN# 0-931334-57-8

CONTENTS

We Remember Roberto

Learn the Key Words

appeal   (ə pēl′)
1. to ask for help
   During the dry spell, Mayor Brook had to <u>appeal</u> to the people to save water.
2. to give pleasure
3. a call for help

athletic   (ath let′ ik)
1. having to do with sports and games
   Barry couldn't decide which <u>athletic</u> event to try out for.
2. active and strong

benefit   (ben′ əɪ fit)
1. to do good; to help
   The new library will <u>benefit</u> all the children in town.
2. anything which is good for a person or thing
3. an act of help or kindness

celebration   (sel ə brā′ shən)   the act of honoring a day or a person with a party or special event
The U.S. honored its 200th birthday with a big <u>celebration</u> in 1976.

horror   (hôr′ ər, hor′ ər)   terror; a feeling of great fear
Les drew back in <u>horror</u> at the sight of the deadly rattlesnake.

memory   (mem′ ər ē)   something that is remembered
The <u>memory</u> of the forest fire reminded the campers to use matches carefully.

Preview:
1. Read the title.
2. Look at the picture.
3. Read the first three paragraphs of the story.
4. Then answer the following question.

You learned from your preview that
_____ a. people were having a Fourth of July party.
_____ b. New Year's Eve is a quiet time in Puerto Rico.
_____ c. the people of Carolina do not own radios.
_____ d. a plane had crashed into the sea.

Turn to the Comprehension Check on page 4 for the right answer.

Now read the story.
Read to find out why so many people admired Roberto Clemente.

We Remember Roberto

*Not just baseball fans will **remember** the great Roberto Clemente.*

Places you will read about:	Puerto Rico (pwer′ tō rē′ kō)	an island southeast of the United States
	Nicaragua (nik ə rä′ gwə)	the largest country in Central America

Things you will read about:	*danzas* (don′ zəs)	a lively type of music that tells of the happiness and sadness of the Puerto Rican people
	National League (nash′ ə nəl lēg)	one of the two big baseball leagues in the United States

Most of the people in the small town of Carolina in Puerto Rico were out in the streets, dancing to gay Spanish music and setting off fireworks. It was New Year's Eve, a time for celebration.

At about four o'clock in the morning, the few people who were still in their homes came out. But it wasn't to join the celebration. With horror on their faces, they sobbed the news:

"The radio just announced that Roberto's plane has crashed into the sea!"

Roberto Clemente was dead. Puerto Rico had lost its national hero. Baseball had lost one of its greatest stars. And the world had lost a generous, loving man

2

who had spent many years helping others.

How far Roberto had come from the time he was a skinny boy hitting tin cans with a broomstick on a dusty Carolina street! He was a quiet, shy boy in school. And how he enjoyed listening to records of Puerto Rico's native music, the *danzas*.

But out on an athletic field, the quiet, shy boy turned into a fiery player. He was an excellent high jumper, and he could throw and hit a softball great distances. The school's athletic coaches recognized sixteen-year-old Roberto's unusual talent and encouraged him to make baseball his future.

After four years with teams in Puerto Rico, Roberto's unusual talent came to the attention of the big league baseball clubs in the United States. In 1954, he was hired by the Pittsburgh Pirates, a last place team. Roberto soon changed it into a winning one.

Roberto's hitting thrilled the Pittsburgh fans. He could hit any kind of pitch thrown to him — inside, outside, or down the middle. Pitchers nearly went crazy trying to figure out what kind of pitch he couldn't hit. In his eighteen years with the Pirates, he collected 3,000 hits; a record held by only ten other men before him in the history of baseball.

In the outfield, Roberto amazed everyone with his throwing arm, an arm that frightened runners on every base. After all, he led the National League five times in throwing base runners out. And how his catches thrilled the fans! Roberto ran into walls and

fences. He dove into the stands. He fell flat on his stomach. He did all this to make catches that seemed impossible.

Off the field, Roberto spent much of his free time working with children. During the winter months, he would return to Puerto Rico and talk to them. He talked about sports, and about being good citizens, and about respecting one's parents.

But Roberto wanted to do more than talk. Roberto had a dream, the dream of building a "Sports City" to benefit the children of Puerto Rico. At Sports City, children would play on the best fields, use the best athletic equipment, and learn from the best coaches. And they would learn to be good citizens. It would cost over two million dollars to build, but it would be free for children.

Sports City became Roberto's life dream. But an earthquake in the Central American country of Nicaragua prevented Roberto from making his dream come true. The earthquake, in December 1972, hit Nicaragua's capital city. Roberto had made many friends there just a few months earlier when the team from Puerto Rico, that he was managing, played the team from Nicaragua's capital in a "little world series."

Roberto immediately began a drive to collect food, clothing, and medicine to benefit the victims of the earthquake. He went on radio to appeal for money. He went from door to door appealing for help.

Soon, $150,000 plus tons of supplies were collected. It was time to send them to Nicaragua. Roberto spent hours at the

airport helping to load the big, four-engine plane. Then, at the last minute, he decided to go along. He wanted to make sure that the supplies reached the victims who needed them most desperately.

Moments after Roberto kissed his wife and three sons good-by, the heavy plane took off from an airport in Puerto Rico. It climbed slowly in the darkness, banking to the left. Then it suddenly crashed into the ocean.

As word spread over the island, thousands of people lined the beaches, watching in horror as boats, planes, and divers searched the heavy seas. Several hours later, the wreck was discovered a mile and a half from shore, buried in 100 feet of water. The pilot's body was found, but Roberto had disappeared without a trace.

In memory of Roberto, tearful people took down their holiday ornaments. They replaced them with black flags. In memory of Roberto, radio stations kept their regular programs from the air. They played only the *danzas* Roberto had loved so much.

And in memory of Roberto, baseball fans all over the world started raising money. They wanted to make his dream of Sports City come true. By March 1975, more than $500,000 had been raised, and building began.

The dream that Roberto couldn't make come true during his lifetime is coming true after his death. Although he is gone, his dream will help others. Through the Roberto Clemente Sports City, the memory of the man who gave everything, including his life, lives on.

We Remember Roberto

Preview answer:
d. a plane had crashed into the sea.

COMPREHENSION CHECK

Choose the best answer.

1. The people of Carolina learned of Roberto's death
   ____ a. in the newspapers.
   ____ b. over the radio.
   ____ c. from his athletic coaches.
   ____ d. from his wife.

2. As a boy in school, Roberto was
   ____ a. quiet and shy.
   ____ b. a national hero.
   ____ c. the class clown.
   ____ d. a big bully.

3. Pitchers had trouble pitching to Roberto because
   ____ a. he was so short.
   ____ b. he never stood still.
   ____ c. he hit all kinds of pitches.
   ____ d. he was very careful.

4. Roberto's strong arm made it easy for him
   ____ a. to fight with other players.
   ____ b. to throw balls to fans in the stands.
   ____ c. to throw base runners out.
   ____ d. to run into walls and fences.

5. Roberto was the kind of ball player who
   ____ a. was interested in setting records.
   ____ b. wouldn't help anyone learn the game.
   ____ c. was always afraid of getting hurt.
   ____ d. gave everything he had to the game.

6. Roberto's life dream was
   ____ a. to be the best player on the Pittsburgh Pirates.
   ____ b. to build a Sports City for children.
   ____ c. to leave Puerto Rico forever.
   ____ d. to discover why earthquakes happened.

7. Roberto's plane crashed
   ____ a. at an airport in Puerto Rico.
   ____ b. in the country of Nicaragua.
   ____ c. near the shore of Puerto Rico.
   ____ d. in the middle of the jungle.

8. Roberto Clemente Sports City was built with money raised by
   ____ a. the Puerto Rican government.
   ____ b. the people of Nicaragua.
   ____ c. the city of Pittsburgh.
   ____ d. baseball fans all over the world.

9. Another name for this story could be
   ____ a. "Puerto Rico's Happy New Year."
   ____ b. "Pittsburgh's Winning Team."
   ____ c. "Victims of the Earthquake."
   ____ d. "A Hero On and Off the Field."

10. This story is mainly about
    ____ a. a baseball player who was hurt many times.
    ____ b. a baseball player who was a star on and off the field.
    ____ c. the training baseball players get in Puerto Rico.
    ____ d. an airplane crash which killed hundreds of people.

Check your answers with the key on page 53.

Idea starter: Who are some other people in whose memory buildings or places have been named?

We Remember Roberto

VOCABULARY CHECK

appeal	athletic	benefit	celebration	horror	memory

I. *Choose the correct key word from the box above to complete each of the following sentences.*

1. Our gym has good _____ equipment.

2. We watched in _____ as the cars crashed.

3. The nation may _____ from a new health program.

4. I have a happy _____ of that party.

5. When our team won, we had a big _____ .

6 In March, the Red Cross will _____ for money.

II. *Choose the word or words with the same meaning as the underlined key word in each sentence. Place an X next to the correct answer.*

1. Mrs. Beck stared in <u>horror</u> as Judy fell from a horse.
   _____ a. Pleasure   _____ b. Terror   _____ c. Pride   _____ d. Hate

2. Hal won a medal for his excellent <u>athletic</u> record.
   _____ a. Successful   _____ b. Stupid   _____ c. Sports   _____ d. Spoil

3. On Veterans Day, we honor the <u>memory</u> of soldiers.
   _____ a. Something forgotten   _____ c. Something written
   _____ b. Something killed   _____ d. Something remembered

4. The new hospital will <u>benefit</u> many people.
   _____ a. Help   _____ b. Halt   _____ c. Worry   _____ d. Frighten

5. The mayor will <u>appeal</u> for votes before Election Day.
   _____ a. Count the numbers   _____ c. Announce the score
   _____ b. Ask for help   _____ d. Threaten the people

6. At Grandpa's birthday <u>celebration</u>, he had 100 candles on his cake.
   _____ a. Honoring party   _____ c. Newspaper story
   _____ b. Ancient building   _____ d. Dreadful disaster

Check your answers with the key on page 55.

This page may be reproduced for classroom use.

The Kidnapping Of Binky Marlowe

Learn the Key Words

astonishment (ə stonʹ ish mənt) great surprise or amazement
He gazed in <u>astonishment</u> at the two-headed dog.

bluff (bluf) to fool someone while acting in a bold manner
He tried to <u>bluff</u> his way into the show without a ticket.

crime (krīm) an unlawful action; wrong-doing
He was sent to prison for the <u>crime</u> of stealing.

dusk (dusk) the darkness after sunset, just before night
When <u>dusk</u> came, we could no longer see the ball and had to stop the game.

ransom (ranʹ səm) a price demanded for the return of someone or something that has been taken without permission
A demand for <u>ransom</u> was sent to the owners of the missing dog.

sip (sip) to drink a little at a time
It is better to <u>sip</u> your milk than to gulp it.

Preview:
1. Read the title.
2. Look at the picture.
3. Read the first paragraph of the story.
4. Then answer the following question.

You learned from your preview that
_____ a. the story begins early in the morning.
_____ b. Binky was at a large shopping center.
_____ c. Binky was interested in a gypsy caravan.
_____ d. Binky was interested in a decorated van.

Turn to the Comprehension Check on page 9 for the right answer.

Now read the story.
Read to find out about Binky's adventures with two strangers.

The Kidnapping Of Binky Marlowe

Binky enjoys adventure – and having her own way.

Something you will read about:	van (van)	a covered truck or wagon

In a parking lot one afternoon, a girl stood staring at a van. In all her ten years, Binky Marlowe had never seen anything so splendid. Bright designs and gay flowers covered its sides. She slowly circled it, wondering who its lucky owners were.

Just then, a man approached, and a smiling woman followed him.

"Would you like to see the inside?" the man asked. "We might have some lemonade," he suggested, as he unlocked the door.

Although Binky had been warned never to go with strangers or accept presents from them, she nodded "Yes."

Inside the van, the woman spoke. "I'm Emma," she said, and invited Binky to sit on a small sofa. Emma filled two glasses with lemonade while the man moved to the front of the van. Just as Binky and the woman started to sip their lemonade, the van began to move.

"I guess Luke wants to show off, so we're going for a ride," Emma said. She looked at Binky, expecting her to be frightened.

"That's all right with me," Binky answered. "I'm always ready for new adventures."

At dusk, Binky yawned and curled up on the sofa. Emma seated herself next to Luke, who was still driving. Certain that

Binky was asleep, they considered the day's happenings.

"Can a ten year old really be so daring?" Emma questioned.

"I think she's trying to bluff us," replied Luke. "Let's get on with our plans to collect some ransom from her family."

"Don't count on ransom," advised a voice from the rear, "because my family doesn't like to spend money."

"We'll decide that for ourselves," said Emma, holding a notebook. "Now, there's no time for nonsense. Just cooperate. What is your family's name, and where do they live?"

"Mr. and Mrs. Benjamin Marlowe, 2000 Shore Drive," was the prompt response from Binky. "But you're headed for trouble. Even if you change your handwriting, your letter can be traced."

"Well, do you think we should telephone them?" asked Luke. "A phone call is easier to track down."

"You certainly are some kidnappers!" Binky exclaimed. "Haven't you ever read adventure stories? You're supposed to cut words out of newspapers to write messages."

"She's right," Emma agreed, "and we'd better do it her way, although it will be an awful lot of work."

"I'll help," offered Binky, "if you get me some scissors."

Luke slammed his hand against the steering wheel. "We may be beginners in crime, but we know what is expected. We cannot allow you to request ransom for yourself."

"You're no fun at all," said Binky, "and I'm sorry I let myself be kidnapped. I told you that I want adventures."

"Well, I believe you," said Emma. "And I also believe that you are a big nuisance. Since we found you at a parking lot, we'll leave you at one. Luke, let's leave her at the next big lot we pass."

Binky was furious. "Just try, and watch what happens to you. If you think you can dump me like old garbage, you're crazy."

"What do you mean?" snapped Luke. "If we leave you at the nearest parking lot, there's nothing you can do about it."

"I'll scream and attract a crowd," threatened Binky. "You can't get rid of me so fast. And there's another thing I want you to know. There are no fresh oranges in your refrigerator."

"Cans of orange juice last longer than fresh oranges," said Emma. "And it's easier to open a can than to squeeze fresh fruit."

"Well, from now on, keep a supply of fresh oranges for me," Binky demanded. "That's the only kind I like!"

"And what would happen if you didn't get them?" Emma wondered.

"Then I wouldn't eat, and I would get thin. I might even die, and remember, causing death is a more serious crime than kidnapping."

Luke was filled with astonishment every time Binky told her kidnappers what to do. By now, he realized that Binky wasn't trying to bluff when she made an announcement.

Long after dusk, Emma and Luke continued making plans, carefully whispering to keep Binky from hearing them.

The next day, Binky was so busy sipping the juice of fresh oranges, planning dinners of her favorite foods, and preparing the letter for ransom, that she never noticed where she was. Suddenly the van stopped, and Emma and Luke hurried out the door, and waited nearby.

Binky glanced through the window and then gasped in astonishment. Here she was, parked in front of her own home. Before a minute had passed, her mother and father had her out of the van and were hugging and kissing her.

"We're delighted to have you home again, Binky!" exclaimed her mother. "We've been terribly worried about you."

"You didn't have to worry, Mother," answered Binky, in a cheerful voice. "You should be delighted that I'll never again go traveling with strangers." As she said this, Binky looked toward Luke and Emma.

Luke and Emma were embarrassed by Binky's scornful gaze. They quickly climbed back into the van and sped away.

"Tomorrow," said Luke, "we'll have to start looking for honest work."

"That's right," agreed Emma. "Now we really know the meaning of that old saying: 'Crime doesn't pay.' "

The Kidnapping Of Binky Marlowe

COMPREHENSION CHECK

Choose the best answer.

1. In the parking lot, Binky saw
    _____ a. a large yellow bus.
    _____ b. a shiny new car.
    _____ c. a brightly colored van.
    _____ d. a crowd of people.

2. Emma and Luke
    _____ a. didn't notice Binky.
    _____ b. invited Binky into their van.
    _____ c. pulled Binky into their van.
    _____ d. asked Binky for directions.

3. Luke
    _____ a. suddenly began to drive the van.
    _____ b. asked Binky where she would like to go.
    _____ c. asked Emma to drive the van.
    _____ d. said that he hated lemonade.

4. Binky said that
    _____ a. she wanted to go home.
    _____ b. she wanted a toothbrush.
    _____ c. she wanted adventures.
    _____ d. she wanted to go shopping.

5. Emma and Luke wanted
    _____ a. to write a letter to Binky.
    _____ b. to telephone Binky's parents.
    _____ c. to leave Binky at a parking lot.
    _____ d. to take Binky for a trip.

6. Binky gasped in astonishment
    _____ a. when she found lemons in the lemonade.
    _____ b. when she found oranges in the refrigerator.
    _____ c. when she found a pair of scissors.
    _____ d. when she found herself at home again.

7. Emma and Luke
    _____ a. were sorry to leave Binky.
    _____ b. loved Binky very much.
    _____ c. would telephone Binky often.
    _____ d. never wanted to see Binky again.

8. After their adventure with Binky, Emma and Luke
    _____ a. wanted to sell their van.
    _____ b. wanted to find honest work.
    _____ c. wanted Binky to live with them.
    _____ d. wanted to drink more lemonade.

9. Another name for this story could be
    _____ a. "Why Fresh Oranges Are Good for Us."
    _____ b. "Binky and Her Friends."
    _____ c. "Two Kidnappers Learn a Lesson."
    _____ d. "Buying a New Van."

10. The main idea of this story is
    _____ a. some people like to visit parking lots.
    _____ b. some girls are quickly frightened.
    _____ c. riding in a van is fun.
    _____ d. two people learned that crime does not pay.

Check your answers with the key on page 53.

Idea starter: Why didn't Emma and Luke collect ransom for Binky?

The Kidnapping Of Binky Marlowe

VOCABULARY CHECK

astonishment	bluff	crime	dusk	ransom	sip

I. Each of the key words has been scrambled. Unscramble each word and write it on the line where it belongs.

1. psi   (drink slowly) _____

2. fulbf   (fool people) _____

3. skud   (when the sun goes down) _____

4. snithmotanse   (amazement) _____

5. mecri   (wrong-doing) _____

6. nasmor   (a price demanded) _____

II. Two key words have been used in each of the following sentences. Make a line through the key word that does <u>not</u> belong in each sentence.

1. I would like to   **bluff sip**   some cold water.

2. His   **astonishment crime**   was punished by the judge.

3. The   **dusk ransom**   made driving difficult.

4. Mr. Howard's scowl is a   **bluff crime;**   he is a very pleasant man.

5. The   **dusk ransom**   was delivered at noon.

6. We tried to hide our   **astonishment sip**   that the lemonade was so **bitter.**

Check your answers with the key on page 55.

The Cleaners

Learn the Key Words

attach (ə tach′)

to fasten; join; connect
Can you attach this rope to the boat?

captive (kap′ tiv)

prisoner
The robber was held captive in a jail cell.

distress (dis tres′)

1. great worry or fear
   His distress was great when his boat began to leak.
2. great pain or suffering

patience (pā′ shəns)

the ability to wait without complaining or growing angry
Rita's patience was exhausted by a long wait in line.

terrify (ter′ ə fī)

to fill with fear; to frighten
The thought of great danger could terrify anyone.

thus (ᴛнus)

1. therefore; accordingly
   We ran fast; thus we were on time.
2. because of this or that

Preview:

1. Read the title.
2. Look at the picture.
3. Read the first two paragraphs of the story.
4. Then answer the following question.

You learned from your preview that
_____ a. all animals often have baths.
_____ b. all animals use their tongues when washing.
_____ c. some animals clean and help each other.
_____ d. only humans clean and help each other.

Turn to the Comprehension Check on page 14 for the right answer.

Now read the story.
Read to find out about some unusual helpers.

The Cleaners

Some animals can keep clean without soap.

Places you will read about:	Africa (af′ rə kə)	one of the seven continents
	Nile River (nīl riv′ ər)	a large river in Africa

Things you will read about:	barracuda (bar ə kü′ də)	a dangerous ocean fish
	plover (pluv′ ər, plō′ vər)	a small bird

As humans, we learn early in life that keeping clean helps keep us healthy. We learn to bathe and brush our teeth. We wash our hands often.

Sometimes it seems that animals, as well as humans, understand that being clean is important. Often one sees an animal, such as a cat, cleaning itself with its tongue. But did you know that animals sometimes clean each other and help each other, much as humans clean and help each other?

"Yes," you may say. "A mother cat cleans her kittens."

But you may be surprised to know that there are also animals who do not belong to the same animal families who clean and help each other in this way.

Far away in Africa, the fierce and dangerous crocodile suns itself on the bank of the Nile River. Crocodiles eat many birds and fish that they capture and swallow whole. Crocodiles are also known as fierce man-eaters, causing distress to any native who comes upon a crocodile by accident. The sight of this animal is enough to terrify a native, and natives kill crocodiles whenever they can.

The African native greatly fears the crocodile, and thus it would seem that little birds and animals would feel the same way. How, then, do we explain the behavior of the "crocodile bird," or plover, who lives along the mud flats of the Nile River? The plover acts, in some ways, as the crocodile's helpful partner. It might be expected that the crocodile would terrify the bird, and yet the crocodile does not.

Small living things attach themselves to the crocodile. The crocodile can't shake off insects, or pick them from its body. But its partner, the plover, likes to eat them. The plover flies down, lands on the crocodile, and feeds. The bird does not show signs of distress. The crocodile lies still and accepts help with great patience.

The crocodile even opens its mouth for the bird. Thus, the plover finds the living things that attach themselves to the crocodile's tongue and gums. The bird flies into the crocodile's mouth to remove harmful bits of animal life. The plover has no fear that the huge mouth will close upon it. If that happened, the bird would be held captive and eaten. The plover satisfies its own hunger while helping the crocodile keep its body free of harmful animal life.

In the sea world, as well as on land, there are other unusual partners who cooperate in a cleaning service. Deep in tropical seas are fish as fierce and dangerous in their territory as the crocodile is in its area. Fish such as sharks and barracudas use their sharp teeth to attack smaller fish before eating them. Yet there are over forty kinds of little "cleaner fish" that are in no fear of these terrors of the sea.

The "cleaner fish" are all brightly colored and easy to spot in the clear seas where they live. They usually stay in rocky areas, almost as if these were their shops for the business of cleaning. Many larger fish swim long distances to . visit the "cleaner fish," and the larger fish wait their turns, much as you would wait in line at a busy store. Each large fish is cleaned in its turn. When the cleaned fish swims away, another fish takes its place. Sometimes the waiting fish show patience, but at other times they are so eager to be next that fights may start.

When the "cleaner fish" is ready to work, it may do a swimming dance around the "customer fish." The customer rests quietly in the water so that it can be worked on. If the customer is very large, several cleaners may share the job.

Just as with a crocodile, tiny pieces of animal life attach themselves to the bodies of the fish. The little "cleaner fish" nibbles away at the scales of the larger fish, eating bits of dirt and attached living things. These become food for the "cleaner fish," as insects do for the plover. If the customer fish has been hurt, the "cleaner fish" eats away the dead flesh, thus cleaning the wound.

Often the customer fish moves its body so the "cleaner fish" can get into some of the areas that are difficult to reach. Sharks have been known to open their mouths and let the "cleaner fish" work all the way down their throats and then swim out again.

As with the plover, the "cleaner fish" has no fear that it will become a captive in the larger animal's mouth. Any other fish would be harmed or eaten. But the "cleaner fish" will be safe. It might seem that sharks and other fierce fish would terrify the cleaners. But they do not.

All through the world there are creatures who help each other. Many living things that serve other living things get something in return. The cleaners are an interesting example of such a group.

As humans, we can understand the need to be clean. And we can appreciate the need of two living beings to cooperate for the advantage of each other.

The Cleaners

COMPREHENSION CHECK

Preview answer:
c. some animals clean and help each other.

Choose the best answer.

1. African natives
   _____ a. love crocodiles.
   _____ b. fear crocodiles.
   _____ c. help crocodiles.
   _____ d. train crocodiles.

2. The plover
   _____ a. fears crocodiles.
   _____ b. avoids crocodiles.
   _____ c. is a crocodile.
   _____ d. helps crocodiles.

3. The plover
   _____ a. warns the natives about crocodiles.
   _____ b. sweeps a crocodile's tail.
   _____ c. brushes a crocodile's teeth.
   _____ d. cleans a crocodile's skin.

4. "Cleaner fish"
   _____ a. clean the ocean floor.
   _____ b. clean the ocean water.
   _____ c. clean the ocean fish.
   _____ d. are cleaner than other fish.

5. "Cleaner fish"
   _____ a. help crocodiles.
   _____ b. bite crocodiles.
   _____ c. help sharks.
   _____ d. fear sharks.

6. The large ocean fish
   _____ a. do not want to be cleaned.
   _____ b. find the "cleaner fish" a nuisance.
   _____ c. keep clean all by themselves.
   _____ d. are eager to be cleaned.

7. The shark does not eat the "cleaner fish" because
   _____ a. the shark is not hungry.
   _____ b. the "cleaner fish" help the shark.
   _____ c. "cleaner fish" don't have a good flavor.
   _____ d. "cleaner fish" swim very fast.

8. The plover and the "cleaner fish"
   _____ a. do the same kind of job.
   _____ b. do different kinds of jobs.
   _____ c. both help crocodiles.
   _____ d. both help ocean fish.

9. Another name for this story could be
   _____ a. "The Sweepers."
   _____ b. "The Dusters."
   _____ c. "The Washers."
   _____ d. "The Helpers."

10. The main idea of this story is
    _____ a. there are some unusual partners in life.
    _____ b. dirty fish sometimes help clean other fish.
    _____ c. dirty crocodiles swim in the Nile River.
    _____ d. plovers and "cleaner fish" have good luck.

Check your answers with the key on page 53.

Idea starter: Name some ways that animals help plants.

The Cleaners

VOCABULARY CHECK

| attach | captive | distress | patience | terrify | thus |

I. Unscramble the key words in BOX I, and write them correctly in BOX II.

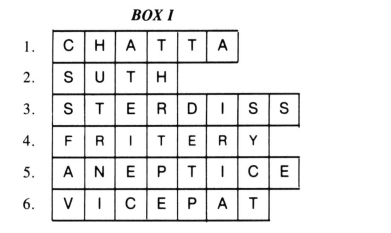

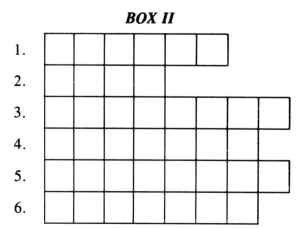

BOX I

1. C H A T T A
2. S U T H
3. S T E R D I S S
4. F R I T E R Y
5. A N E P T I C E
6. V I C E P A T

BOX II

1.
2.
3.
4.
5.
6.

II. Now use the words from BOX II to fill in the blanks in the following sentences.

1. Insects _____ themselves to crocodiles.

2. She wanted to do well, and _____ she worked very hard.

3. The shark causes _____ to many fish in the sea.

4. That sudden, loud sound could _____ a person!

5. He showed great _____ when asked to wait an hour longer.

6. When he heard the door being locked, he knew he was a _____ .

Check your answers with the key on page 56.

The Passenger Pigeon

Learn the Key Words

breed (brēd) produce more of one's kind; have babies
The buffalo didn't breed fast enough to replace those killed.

brilliant (bril′ yənt) shining; brightly colored
The woodpecker's head was a brilliant shade of red.

glorious (glôr′ ē əs) famous; wonderful
The tall ships sailing along the coast were a glorious sight.

limit (lim′ it) where something ends
We are discovering that there is a limit to our fuel supplies.

total (tō′ tl) all; the whole amount of
The total rainfall in the desert is near zero.

twig (twig) a very small branch on a tree
When a twig breaks off a tree, a scar may remain.

Preview:
1. Read the title.
2. Look at the picture.
3. Read the first paragraph.
4. Then answer the following question.

You learned from your preview that
_____ a. North America once had millions and millions of passenger pigeons.
_____ b. Europe once had millions and millions of passenger pigeons.
_____ c. passenger pigeons were first noticed around 1900.
_____ d. the large number of passenger pigeons was a secret.

Turn to the Comprehension Check on page 19 for the right answer.

Now read the story.
Read to find out why we no longer see passenger pigeons.

The Passenger Pigeon

Flocks of these birds could quickly strip a field of grain.

A place you will read about:	Montreal (mon trē ôl′)	a large city in Canada

People you will read about:	John Jacob Audubon (jon jā′ kəb ô′ də bon)	an American painter who studied birds
	Alexander Wilson (al ig zan′ dər wil′ sən)	a man who studied birds and made pictures of them

Once there were millions and millions of passenger pigeons in North America. The early settlers could hardly believe the size of the flocks they saw. When they wrote to Europe, they told their friends that there was no limit to the number of pigeons. They wrote about the flights of birds that filled the skies for miles. The Europeans found it hard to believe that there were such glorious flights of birds anywhere. No one in Europe had ever seen such a sight.

An American observer of nature, Alexander Wilson, wrote in 1810 that he saw a flock of over two thousand million birds. He wrote that the flock was so thick that it darkened the sky from horizon to horizon for four hours. He said the birds flew past him at sixty miles an hour. They were flying faster than most cars travel on our highways today.

The flocks were so huge and glorious that people in America

thought that these birds would be here forever. But now the great mass of pigeons has disappeared. There are no passenger pigeons left anywhere in the world.

What happened to them?

One trouble was that it took so much food to keep the huge flocks alive. They ate berries, small fruit, acorns, and other nuts. But sometimes they ate the farmers' grain. Alexander Wilson figured that the tremendous flock of pigeons that he saw would eat a total of 17½ million bushels of grain in one day. At that time there were only about six million people in the United States. Wilson's flock could eat more grain in a day than the entire population of the country would eat in a year!

Naturally, the farmers in the United States and Canada were very unhappy to see such huge flights land in the woods near their fields. Near Montreal, Canada, in 1687 the number of pigeons was enormous. They ate so much grain that the farmers considered them evil beings. They asked their church leaders to get rid of the pigeons with specially blessed waters.

Wherever the great flights traveled, they frightened some people with their huge numbers that darkened the skies for hours. They were not flying to find a different climate. They were simply searching for food. When the pigeons discovered enough food, they would land on all of the trees in the neighborhood. Every twig on every branch became a landing place. Sometimes so many birds landed on a single branch that

the branch broke. Sometimes an entire tree would be stripped of every twig by the weight of the passenger pigeons.

Although the pigeons ate a lot, they were also good to eat. They were good-sized birds with heavy bodies. Counting their eight-inch tails, the male pigeons were about seventeen inches long. The males were colored dark blue above and deep red below. Their necks were brilliant shades of shining colors. The females were not so brilliant. They were smaller and less colorful.

The early settlers found both the males and females very tasty. At first they would eat what birds they could and preserve a few barrels of pigeons to help feed their families through the long winters.

Then the trains came along. There seemed to be no limit to the number of birds that the railroad cars could carry for sale in New York and Boston and other eastern cities. John Jacob Audubon, a famous student of nature and painter of birds, reported that in 1805 he saw ships in New York's harbor loaded with pigeons to be sold in Europe for one cent each.

Hundreds of thousands of live pigeons were captured. Many thousands were kept in cages and fattened for the market. Other live pigeons were used in "trap shooting." These pigeons would be let out of traps and then shot by men with guns. Finally the public was angered and put a stop to this cruel sport.

But the public could not save the glorious pigeons that thrilled people in North America for

nearly three hundred years. One reason was that their number was so tremendous. People did not think that they would ever disappear from the skies. However, the female pigeons would breed only once a year. They would lay only one or two eggs at a time. This rate of breeding was not enough to make up for the total number of birds killed every year.

About one hundred years ago, some people began to doubt that the pigeons would thrive much longer. But every year millions of birds were still reported. Most people thought that there was just no limit to their numbers. When one of the great flocks was reported, people would come from miles around to kill the birds by the thousands. Some came just to watch the killing. The number of wild pigeons was dropping rapidly.

The last glorious gathering of pigeons — at least one hundred million birds — was last seen in Michigan in 1878. About twenty years later the last wild passenger pigeon was killed. The brilliant flashing flights were seen no more.

In 1914, in a Cincinnati zoo, a bird named Martha died at the age of twenty-nine. She was the last passenger pigeon in the entire world.

The Passenger Pigeon

COMPREHENSION CHECK

Preview answer:

a. North American once had millions and millions of passenger pigeons.

Choose the best answer.

1. The passenger pigeon was
   _____ a. brought to America from Europe.
   _____ b. a native American bird.
   _____ c. always a rare bird.
   _____ d. killed for its brilliant feathers.

2. Because there were so many passenger pigeons in 1810, people thought that
   _____ a. they would scare the little children.
   _____ b. they would be here forever.
   _____ c. they would frighten the other birds away.
   _____ d. a national park should be set aside for them.

3. There were so many pigeons in some flights that
   _____ a. they darkened the skies for hours.
   _____ b. they kept crashing into each other.
   _____ c. they frightened the settlers back to Europe.
   _____ d. they prevented the crops from getting rain.

4. One of the largest flights reported had at least
   _____ a. several hundred birds.
   _____ b. several thousand birds.
   _____ c. a million birds.
   _____ d. many millions of birds.

5. The early settlers found that the pigeons ate
   _____ a. fish and small game.
   _____ b. only nuts and berries.
   _____ c. their grain crops.
   _____ d. mostly insects.

6. The weight of a flock of pigeons often
   _____ a. broke in the settlers' roofs.
   _____ b. broke the twigs off trees.
   _____ c. caused landslides.
   _____ d. crushed the grain fields.

7. The last flock of passenger pigeons was seen
   _____ a. in Michigan about one hundred years ago.
   _____ b. in a zoo in Europe.
   _____ c. in Montreal, Canada, a few years ago.
   _____ d. in California during a snow storm.

8. The saddest fact about the passenger pigeon is that
   _____ a. it ate so many berries.
   _____ b. it used to darken the skies.
   _____ c. it broke down so many trees.
   _____ d. it is no longer living.

9. Another name for this story could be
   _____ a. "The Most Brilliant Birds in America."
   _____ b. "The Last of the Wild Animals."
   _____ c. "The Greatest Flocks That Ever Flew.'
   _____ d. "The Bird They Could Not Tame."

10. This story is mainly about
    _____ a. a kind of wild bird.
    _____ b. the food of the early settlers.
    _____ c. the largest bird that ever flew.
    _____ d. how to breed pigeons.

Check your answers with the key on page 53.

Idea starter: Name some other wild animals that may disappear forever if people do not protect them.

The Passenger Pigeon

VOCABULARY CHECK

breed	brilliant	glorious	limit	total	twig

I. *Choose the best key word from the box to complete each sentence. Each word should be used only once.*

1. What is the speed _____ in a school zone?

2. After the rain, the grass was a _____ shade of green.

3. Helen paid a _____ of ten dollars for what she bought.

4. Rabbits produce many young because they _____ often.

5. A statue was built to honor the _____ hero.

6. The robin flew to the highest _____ on the apple tree.

II. *Use the key words in the box above to complete the puzzle.*

Across

2. Full of glory
3. Full of light
5. The smallest branch

Down

1. The whole amount
3. Give birth
4. Where something ends

Check your answers with the key on page 56.

This page may be reproduced for classroom use.

The Loch Ness Monster

Learn the Key Words

aware	(ə wer′, ə war′)	knowing; having knowledge *She was <u>aware</u> of pain when she cut her finger.*
cautious	(kô′ shəs)	careful *You should be <u>cautious</u> when you cross the street.*
inhabitant	(in hab′ ə tənt)	a person who lives in a certain area or place *Each of us is an <u>inhabitant</u> of our town or city.*
ridiculous	(ri dik′ yə ləs)	foolish; doesn't make sense *We laughed at John's <u>ridiculous</u> attempt to fly.*
theory	(thē′ ər ē, thir′ ē)	an idea or opinion *The scientist's <u>theory</u> was tested many times.*
visible	(viz′ ə bəl)	can be seen; plain to see *The sea is <u>visible</u> from this window.*

Preview:
1. Read the title.
2. Look at the picture.
3. Read the first paragraph of the story.
4. Then answer the following question.

You learned from your preview that
_____ a. a monster is living in Scotland.
_____ b. the monster's nickname is Loch Ness.
_____ c. the monster's nickname is Nessie.
_____ d. very few people know about the monster.

Turn to the Comprehension Check on page 24 for the right answer.

Now read the story.
Read to find some strange reports about a lake in Scotland.

The Loch Ness Monster

This lake may be the home of a monster.

A place you will read about:	Loch Ness	(lok nes′)	a lake in northern Scotland

In a deep, dark lake in northern Scotland, a monster may be living. The lake is called Loch Ness, and the monster is called the Loch Ness Monster. The monster's nickname is "Nessie." Nessie is the world's most famous monster. It is also one of the most bewildering and amazing puzzles of the world.

Many people think that the idea of a monster living in a lake is ridiculous. But, an inhabitant of a town near the lake wouldn't think so. People living near the lake have been aware of reports of the Loch Ness Monster for a

long time. The reports date back to the sixth century. At that time, a monk living at the western side of the lake thought he saw a monster. It appeared to be a huge worm that rose above the water.

Since that time, the monster has been seen by many different people. One guess is that about 3000 people have seen it. Many of these people were not inhabitants of the area. They were people who visited the lake from all parts of the world.

Many inhabitants of the lake region have probably seen the

monster. But, those people are cautious when talking to strangers about it. They are aware that some people scorn the idea of the Loch Ness Monster. They don't want to appear ridiculous. So, the inhabitants discuss it only with each other.

A monster that has been visible to so many people for so long cannot be ignored. The world really started paying attention to Nessie in 1933. Then, a new road was built along the northern shore of the lake. The lake was now more visible to people. Suddenly more and more people caught glimpses of a monster in Loch Ness. One theory is that the monster rose above the water to see what all the noise was about. Usually, noise made the monster hide. Nessie was supposed to be timid. But, the noise from the road construction might have made Nessie curious.

The following year, a man with a camera snapped the first picture of Nessie. Now more people started believing that Nessie was real. Others were still cautious. They said that no such thing as a monster lived in Loch Ness or in any other lake. They said that the picture must be a trick or a joke.

The picture was printed in newspapers all over the world. People grew excited at the thought that the monster could possibly be real. People started asking questions. If there really were a monster in Loch Ness, what kind is it? Nearly all of the people who thought they had seen Nessie offered different descriptions. No one had ever seen anything like it before.

Different sizes, shapes, and colors were reported. Some people had seen a long tail. Others had not seen any tail. Some had seen only a long neck. Others had seen growths spreading from the sides of the body. Scientists can't say to which family the monster belongs. Is it a fish, a dinosaur, or a serpent? Today the most popular theory is that Nessie is a sea-going dinosaur.

All these different kinds of stories led to another theory. There must be more than one monster in the lake. After all,

the original Nessie would have to be 5000 years old. Scientists agree that no creature could live so long. The monster in the legend must be an ancestor of today's Nessies.

Where, then, were all the old Nessies? Scientists thought the dead monsters must be at the bottom of the lake. The lake has no tides strong enough to wash the bodies to the shore.

People said that sea creatures, like Nessie, couldn't live in a fresh-water lake. Scientists said that, indeed, there were some kinds of sea creatures that could. Nessie and its family must be one of them.

People wanted to know how Nessie got into the lake in the first place. Scientists said that Loch Ness was once part of the sea. During the last Ice Age, the shifting lands made the lake we call Loch Ness and trapped Nessie within it.

People asked why the monster was visible only at certain times. Scientists answered that there might be caves where it hides. Or, Nessie might swim in and out of the lake through passages on the bottom of the lake.

People have searched for Nessie since its first picture was shown to the world. More glimpses have been reported, and more pictures have been taken. Some people have joined expeditions using special equipment to see or hear Nessie. Others have gone alone with only cameras or special glasses. No one has been able to prove that the monster is real.

A new picture of Nessie, taken in 1975, led to a new expedition. Equipped with the

most modern gear, a group left the United States for Loch Ness. This group was determined to solve the mystery of the Loch Ness Monster. By September 1976, Nessie had neither been seen nor heard from.

Is it because there is no such thing as the Loch Ness Monster? Or, is it because Nessie is hiding at the bottom of the lake? The mystery continues, and so does the search.

The Loch Ness Monster

COMPREHENSION CHECK

Choose the best answer.

1. The Loch Ness Monster is supposed
   _____ a. to live in the ocean.
   _____ b. to live in a village.
   _____ c. to live in a lake.
   _____ d. to live on a boat.

2. The legend of the Loch Ness Monster
   _____ a. has been known for a few years.
   _____ b. has been known since 1933.
   _____ c. has been known for centuries.
   _____ d. has been known since 1975.

3. The Loch Ness Monster is supposed to have been seen
   _____ a. only by tourists to Scotland.
   _____ b. only by inhabitants of the Loch Ness area.
   _____ c. by almost 3000 people.
   _____ d. only before 1933.

4. The inhabitants around Loch Ness
   _____ a. love to talk about the monster to strangers.
   _____ b. don't believe that there is a monster.
   _____ c. think the Loch Ness legend is ridiculous.
   _____ d. don't like to talk to strangers about the monster.

5. Almost everyone who saw the Loch Ness Monster
   _____ a. agreed that it was a fish.
   _____ b. agreed that it was a dinosaur.
   _____ c. agreed that it was a serpent.
   _____ d. described something different.

6. The most popular theory is that
   _____ a. the monster is a kind of fish.
   _____ b. the monster is a kind of whale.
   _____ c. the monster is a kind of dinosaur.
   _____ d. the monster is a kind of snake.

7. Some scientists have a theory that
   _____ a. there are many monsters in the lake.
   _____ b. the monster is 5000 years old.
   _____ c. there was a monster, but now it is gone.
   _____ d. it is impossible for a monster to live in Loch Ness.

8. The Loch Ness Monster
   _____ a. is only a fairy tale.
   _____ b. couldn't possibly be real.
   _____ c. must have died years ago.
   _____ d. might possibly be real.

9. Another name for this story could be
   _____ a. ''Fishing in Scotland.''
   _____ b. ''The Mystery of Loch Ness.''
   _____ c. ''The History of Scotland.''
   _____ d. ''Beautiful Scottish Lakes.''

10. The main idea of this story is
    _____ a. there is no proof of the Loch Ness Monster.
    _____ b. no one wants to find the Loch Ness Monster.
    _____ c. no one believes there is a Loch Ness Monster.
    _____ d. there are no pictures of the Loch Ness Monster.

Check your answers with the key on page 53.

Idea starter: Should people keep searching for the Loch Ness Monster? Why?

The Loch Ness Monster

VOCABULARY CHECK

aware	cautious	inhabitant	ridiculous	theory	visible

I. **Write the correct key word from the box above in each of the following blanks.**

1. Your garden is _____ again. The fog has disappeared.

2. You are an _____ of this town. You have lived here many years.

3. Your _____ was a good one. It has been proven to be correct!

4. You are not _____ that the rain has stopped. Your umbrella is still open.

5. You are _____ when carrying the vase. You don't want to drop it.

6. You felt _____ when you sat down. Everyone laughed when you missed the chair!

II. **Put an X next to the best answer for each sentence.**

1. If a story is <u>ridiculous</u>,
   _____ a. you would believe it.
   _____ b. you would laugh at it.

2. If you are <u>aware</u> of something,
   _____ a. you know it.
   _____ b. you hold it.

3. If you had a <u>theory</u> about something,
   _____ a. you would have proof.
   _____ b. you would try to find proof.

4. If something is <u>visible</u>,
   _____ a. you can see it.
   _____ b. you can't see it.

5. If you are an <u>inhabitant</u> of a place,
   _____ a. you visit there.
   _____ b. you live there.

6. If you are <u>cautious</u> when carrying something,
   _____ a. you would want to drop it.
   _____ b. you wouldn't want to drop it.

Check your answers with the key on page 57.

This page may be reproduced for classroom use.

"Tell Us Why, Peter"

Learn the Key Words

fury (fyu̇r′ ē) great anger
He was filled with fury when he knew that they had fooled him.

marvel (mär′ vəl) to be filled with wonder
I marvel at the way she does those tricks without a single mistake.

miracle (mir′ ə kəl) an amazing and unusual event
It was a miracle that they escaped being hurt in that fire.

numb (num) having no feeling, as when parts of the body are very cold
When my fingers and toes are numb, I know it's time to go home.

rely (ri lī′) to depend on; to trust
You know you can rely on me to be there when you need me.

strife (strīf) a struggle or quarrel
The strife between the two nations led to war.

Preview:

1. Read the title.
2. Look at the picture.
3. Read the first paragraph of the story.
4. Then answer the following question.

You learned from your preview that
_____ a. the story takes place in Prussia.
_____ b. the story takes place in summer.
_____ c. people didn't like the beginning of winter.
_____ d. people celebrated the beginning of winter.

Turn to the Comprehension Check on page 29 for the right answer.

Now read the story.
Read to find out how one family started a new season.

"Tell Us Why, Peter"

Peter does not believe that his family's dreams will come true.

> *Things you will read about:*
> | | | |
> |---|---|---|
> | Archangel Gabriel | (ärk' ān jəl gā' brē əl) | an angel who acts as God's messenger |
> | icon | (ī' kon) | a picture of a holy person, often painted on wood |

In a small town in Russia, in 1880, the start of each new season was celebrated as if it were a miracle. Even the long, hard winter received a merry welcome. The first snow brought people outside, clothed in rags, leathers, and furs. Looking as fat, clumsy bears do, they strolled through the town. An ice slide was built near the market, and gay flags fluttered from its wooden beams.

But one boy, named Peter, did not marvel at that year's first snow.

Carefully, he touched the stone heating in the large, brick oven of his family's two-room home. The stone was still not hot enough. Peter hugged himself as gusts of wind found their way through the wooden walls. His finger tips felt numb. "The first snow," he thought. "Why isn't Michael home yet? Olga needs her husband at a time like this."

A moan from behind his sister's closed door wrapped itself around Peter's heart and squeezed tightly. Peter faced his family's icons and placed his one small candle before the Archangel Gabriel.

"Blessed Gabriel," he whispered, "please ask our Lord to let Olga have this baby. Don't let another one die. Please."

Peter brushed tears from his cheeks and grabbed a clean rag to wrap around the warm stone. ''Twelve years old,'' he muttered to himself, ''and this is all I'm good for: praying, crying, and heating stones.''

Carrying the wrapped stone, he knocked softly at the bedroom door. His mother poked her head out, took the warm stone, and closed the door quickly. A moment later, the door opened again and she slipped out. Peter searched her face for a sign of how things were going, but it was not Olga his mother was thinking of just then. Pressing both hands to her side, she began to cough and sat down heavily before the warm oven.

''The first snow,'' she sighed. ''I don't need it to announce that winter is here. I cough in winter like a rooster crows at dawn. No sign of Michael yet?''

Peter shook his head.

''The river must be choked with ice,'' his mother said. ''How long will it take for the boats to push through?''

''Is there anything I can do?'' Peter asked.

''Study your books,'' his mother answered. ''Tell us why our lives are so full of strife. Why can't Michael be here now when Olga needs him?'' Still muttering, she returned to her daughter.

Peter kicked the oven in fury. Everyone was needed, except him. In times of strife, everyone could rely on everyone else, but they would not rely on him. He was strong, and willing to work

on the riverboats as Michael did. But no, he was only allowed to study. The dreams his family had for him: to attend the university, to become a doctor. It was impossible, crazy! And they needed money so badly now.

Peter's fury raged on as he recalled how they had trapped him when he was a very small child. Long ago, his widowed mother had taken him along when she worked for Mr. Ivanov, a rich merchant. Mr. Ivanov's daughter, Anna, amused herself by reading to Peter while his mother did the family's wash. Then, one day, to everyone's astonishment, three-year-old Peter began reading back. Then and there his life was planned for him.

''Read, Peter. Study, Peter. Become a doctor, Peter. Tell us why your sister's babies die. Tell us why your mother coughs blood. Tell us why your father died when he was only forty. Tell us why, Peter, and tell us how to make life better.''

''In twenty years, maybe I'll know what to tell them,'' Peter thought desperately, ''but what good will it do? They'll all be starved, frozen, sick, or dead.''

The front door groaned on its hinges, and Michael rushed in with the bitter wind. ''Where's Olga?'' he gasped.

''Calm yourself, Michael,'' Peter said, hugging his brother-in-law. ''She'll need you to be calm. She's in the bedroom.''

Michael moved toward the oven, holding out his red, numb hands to be warmed. Then Olga suddenly cried out, and he rushed inside to her.

Peter faced the icons. ''Let the baby live. Please let it live. Please . . .''

As Peter prayed, his mother appeared beside him. Her tired eyes told him no more than ''Go in'' before they fixed themselves on the icons.

Peter approached the open door, his throat sore with fear.

The baby, a girl, was smaller than he had expected, and redder, and much, much uglier. His face must have shown his feelings, because Michael laughed loudly. The baby in Olga's arms howled in surprise.

Hearing her cry, Peter felt something different and new: an aching feeling as if his heart were straining out to touch the baby. ''Don't cry,'' he murmured. ''I don't want you ever to cry. Life must be better for you.''

Suddenly, Peter understood why his family pressed him to study. Money, food, medicine — yes, they needed them all. But, hope for the future! Hope, a miracle as great as his tiny niece, a miracle as fresh as the first snow, they needed even more.

Leaving Olga and the baby to rest, Peter raced his brother-in-law through the snow, ready at last to marvel at the start of a new season.

"Tell Us Why, Peter"

COMPREHENSION CHECK

Choose the best answer.

1. Peter lived
    _____ a. in a small town in Russia.
    _____ b. in an apartment house.
    _____ c. in a big city.
    _____ d. near the ocean.

2. This story takes place
    _____ a. in the present, about last Tuesday.
    _____ b. in the future, about 2080.
    _____ c. in the past, about a hundred years ago.
    _____ d. in 1968.

3. The people of the town
    _____ a. were afraid of winter.
    _____ b. celebrated the start of each new season.
    _____ c. did not like snow.
    _____ d. celebrated everything except winter.

4. Peter was worried about
    _____ a. the snow.
    _____ b. not knowing how to read.
    _____ c. his sister and her baby.
    _____ d. the celebration.

5. Michael was not home because
    _____ a. he was working on a riverboat.
    _____ b. he was at the celebration.
    _____ c. he was lost.
    _____ d. he was afraid.

6. Peter's family wanted him
    _____ a. to work on a riverboat.
    _____ b. to become a doctor.
    _____ c. to go to the celebration.
    _____ d. to get a job right away.

7. Peter wished he could
    _____ a. go to school.
    _____ b. run away.
    _____ c. have a vacation.
    _____ d. work on a riverboat.

8. The baby and the new season were alike because
    _____ a. they both brought new hope for the future.
    _____ b. Peter didn't like them.
    _____ c. nobody cared about them.
    _____ d. they both were unhappy.

9. Another name for this story could be
    _____ a. "Peter Gets a Job."
    _____ b. "Danger on a Riverboat."
    _____ c. "A Season of Hope."
    _____ d. "Peter's Sister."

10. This story is mainly about
    _____ a. a winter celebration.
    _____ b. poor people hoping for a better future.
    _____ c. a man who works on a boat.
    _____ d. a boy who doesn't like school.

Check your answers with the key on page 53.

Idea starter: Why did Peter tell the baby, "Life must be better for you"?

"Tell Us Why, Peter"

VOCABULARY CHECK

fury	marvel	miracle	numb	rely	strife

I. **Fill in the blank in each sentence with the correct key word from the box above.**

1. Because of labor _____ , the factory was closed.

2. We _____ at Sue's knowledge of history.

3. Roger turned red with _____ when he lost his money.

4. Before you _____ on those tires, be sure they have no leaks.

5. Jerry knew that a _____ was needed for his team to win.

6. I soaked my _____ feet in warm water.

II. **Write a key word from the box next to its meaning.**

1. _____ having no feeling

2. _____ great anger

3. _____ to depend on

4. _____ a struggle or quarrel

5. _____ to be filled with wonder

6. _____ an astonishing event

Check your answers with the key on page 57.

The Real Sherlock Holmes

Learn the Key Words

admiration	(ad mə rā′ shən)	a feeling of wonder and approval
		The public felt admiration for Sherlock Holmes.
chemistry	(kem′ ə strē)	the science that deals with the composition and changes of matter
		A knowledge of chemistry is needed to make many new materials.
disguise	(dis gīz′)	to change appearance to prevent being recognized
		The young man used to disguise himself with a beard.
fabulous	(fab′ yə ləs)	marvelous; amazing
		The sun may become a fabulous source of energy.
laboratory	(lab′ rə tôr ə)	a place where experiments are performed
		The human hairs were taken to a laboratory for examination.
sergeant	(sär′ jənt)	a person who holds a position of command in the army or police
		The sergeant ordered the soldiers to get haircuts.

Preview:
1. Read the title.
2. Look at the picture.
3. Read the first two paragraphs of the story.
4. Then answer the following question.

You learned from your preview that
_____ a. Sherlock Holmes wrote about Arthur Conan Doyle.
_____ b. Sherlock Holmes was dreamed up for television.
_____ c. Sherlock Holmes first appeared more than sixty years ago.
_____ d. Sherlock Holmes manages a laboratory for the police.

Turn to the Comprehension Check on page 34 for the right answer.

Now read the story.
Read to find out who the model for Sherlock Holmes was.

The Real Sherlock Holmes

This famous detective was born in a doctor's office.

The most famous detective of all time was Sherlock Holmes. Of course, he never really lived. He is a character in a series of mystery tales by Sir Arthur Conan Doyle. These stories have been admired all over the world for their clever detective work. Years ago, these tales were studied by police everywhere. In some cities, Sherlock Holmes's work was even copied in the police laboratory.

The last Sherlock Holmes story was written more than sixty years ago. We still think of him with admiration. He was dreamed up by Conan Doyle when Doyle was a young doctor in England. The doctor had very few patients. To give himself something to do and to earn some money, he started writing his stories about the tall detective and his fat friend, the faithful Dr. Watson.

At first Doyle modeled Holmes after his college teacher, Dr. Joseph Bell. Bell used the discoveries of chemistry laboratories as well as his own fabulous ability to observe. He showed his students that they must use their eyes and ears carefully. He would look at a new patient and say, "This man is left-handed, and he makes shoes for a living." Then he would point out to his surprised students the worn place on the man's pants. The worn place showed where the man held the shoes that he worked on. Since the worn place was on the right side, the man must have held his hammer in his left hand. The students shook their heads in wonder and said that their teacher could observe details better than any police sergeant.

The first Sherlock Holmes story was "A Study in Scarlet," written in 1886. Two magazines refused the story before another accepted it. The story was then held for several months before it was printed. But soon Sherlock Holmes had become a famous character. The public admired him so much that the magazines demanded more and more Holmes stories from Conan Doyle. The great success of these stories and the fabulous sums of money that they brought Doyle made him a man of great wealth. He gave up his practice as a doctor and devoted himself entirely to writing stories.

Years passed, and Doyle grew tired of writing tales about Holmes and Dr. Watson and police sergeants. Because he wanted to write serious books, Doyle grew annoyed with the world's admiration for his detective. So he decided to kill Sherlock Holmes. He wrote a story in which Holmes and his enemy, Professor Moriarty, fought at the top of a high cliff. The two men, locked in each other's arms in a fierce struggle, fell to their deaths in the water far below.

The public would not accept this death for their hero. After ten years, Conan Doyle had to bring Sherlock Holmes back to life. He explained in a new story that Holmes had escaped by climbing up the face of a steep cliff.

Although Conan Doyle never stated publicly that he really modeled Holmes after himself, we can now be sure that he did. Two different times in real life, Doyle used his detective abilities to put together the facts to free men from prison. He proved that the two men were innocent of the crimes they had been charged with. One was a black man named Edalji. He had been sent to prison for the cruel killings of animals on nearby farms. Doyle was convinced that Edalji had been arrested and tried mostly because he behaved strangely and because he was black. Working as his famous detective did, Doyle proved that another man had committed the crimes.

The second man that Doyle cleared was Oscar Slater. Slater had been sent to prison for robbing a wealthy old woman and killing her with a hammer. Doyle uncovered evidence that proved that Slater was not guilty.

In describing Holmes, Doyle gave him some of his own ways and habits. He had Holmes wear a dressing gown like his own, and smoke a pipe like the one he used. He gave Holmes his own interest in chemistry and other sciences. Holmes and Doyle both treated women with unusually great respect. In their early days in London, both men struggled with poverty. They even lived on the same street. Doyle even gave Holmes his own kind of ancestors, including a French grandmother. In the story "His Last Bow," when Holmes was in disguise, he used the name Altamont, the middle name of Doyle's own father.

There are books that explain how much Holmes was like the author. In *The Life of Sir Arthur Conan Doyle: The Man Who Was Sherlock Holmes*, John Dickson Carr says that Doyle was very much surprised that the public could never see through the thin disguise.

Probably the best evidence that Doyle was Holmes are the words of his widow. After her husband's death, she wrote an article called "Conan Doyle Was Sherlock Holmes." She told about his solving mysteries that the police could not solve. She wrote: "The public does not realize that my husband had the Sherlock Holmes brain."

The Real Sherlock Holmes

COMPREHENSION CHECK

Choose the best answer.

1. The most famous detective in the world was
   ____ a. Sir Arthur Conan Doyle.
   ____ b. a police sergeant.
   ____ c. Dr. John Watson.
   ____ d. Sherlock Holmes.

2. Arthur Conan Doyle was
   ____ a. a police sergeant.
   ____ b. a doctor.
   ____ c. a chemistry teacher.
   ____ d. a lawyer.

3. The first model for Sherlock Holmes was
   ____ a. the author himself.
   ____ b. Dr. John Watson.
   ____ c. a college professor.
   ____ d. a famous detective.

4. "A Study in Scarlet" is
   ____ a. a poem by Conan Doyle.
   ____ b. a true story.
   ____ c. the first Sherlock Holmes story.
   ____ d. the last Sherlock Holmes story.

5. The Sherlock Holmes stories
   ____ a. made Conan Doyle famous.
   ____ b. were laughed at by real policemen.
   ____ c. were really written by Dr. Joseph Bell.
   ____ d. were disliked at first by readers.

6. In one story, Conan Doyle
   ____ a. made Sherlock Holmes a doctor.
   ____ b. disguised Holmes as a woman.
   ____ c. admitted that he was Holmes.
   ____ d. had Sherlock Holmes fall to his death.

7. In real life, Conan Doyle
   ____ a. often dressed up as Sherlock Holmes.
   ____ b. solved two famous crimes.
   ____ c. kept up his practice as a doctor.
   ____ d. was never a poor man.

8. A character in a story
   ____ a. is never based on a real person.
   ____ b. is always a real person.
   ____ c. can become more famous than a real person.
   ____ d. can never be forgotten.

9. Another name for this story could be
   ____ a. "Dr. Bell's Invention."
   ____ b. "The Real Murderer."
   ____ c. "The Writer Who Wrote about Himself."
   ____ d. "The Death of Sir Arthur."

10. This story is mainly about
    ____ a. two real-life murders.
    ____ b. a struggle with poverty.
    ____ c. the ability to observe details.
    ____ d. a famous writer.

Check your answers with the key on page 53.

Idea starter: Why are some books that were written many years ago still popular today?

The Real Sherlock Holmes

VOCABULARY CHECK

admiration	chemistry	disguise	fabulous	laboratory	sergeant

I. Choose the best key word from the box above to complete each sentence.

1. I don't believe his _____ stories are true.

2. My brother was made a police _____ .

3. We have great _____ for brave people.

4. The wonder drug was developed in a _____ .

5. Is a stocking mask a good _____ ?

6. The girls made salt in their _____ laboratory.

II. Two key words have been used in each of the following sentences. Make a line through the key word that does __not__ belong in each sentence.

1. His **admiration fabulous** for the hero made him cheer.

2. The **laboratory sergeant** glowed with good health.

3. A **chemistry fabulous** experiment led to the discovery of America.

4. Her **admiration laboratory** is large and modern.

5. My **disguise sergeant** kept me from being recognized.

6. That **chemistry disguise** class is for science students.

Check your answers with the key on page 58.

It's Not the Worst Thing in the World

Learn the Key Words

challenge   (chal′ ənj)   something especially difficult or unusual; something that requires a special effort
> *Playing basketball against the champion team will be a real <u>challenge</u> for us.*

choice   (chois)   someone or something that has been chosen
> *She is our <u>choice</u> for class president.*

expression   (ek spresh′ ən)   a look on a person's face that shows how one feels
> *I could tell by the <u>expression</u> on his face that he was very angry.*

glimpse   (glimps)   a quick look
> *The car was speeding, but I did get a <u>glimpse</u> of the driver.*

graceful   (grās′ fəl)   full of charm and beauty; moving easily
> *We all admire Cheryl's <u>graceful</u> dancing.*

terrific   (tə rif′ ik)   wonderful; exciting
> *What <u>terrific</u> skaters they are!*

Preview:
1. Read the title.
2. Look at the picture.
3. Read the first two paragraphs of the story.
4. Then answer the following question.

You learned from your preview that
_____ a. the story begins on the first day of school.
_____ b. a boy has joined the class during the year.
_____ c. a play has been written about Red Riding Hood.
_____ d. a boy doesn't want to help with a class play.

Turn to the Comprehension Check on page 39 for the right answer.

Now read the story.
Read to find out what happens to a terrific idea.

It's Not the Worst Thing in the World

Unless Rick thinks fast, he won't be included in the school play.

Something you will read about:
tape recorder   (tāp′ ri kôr′ dər)   a machine that records sound and plays back the sound

---

It's not the worst thing in the world to be the new boy in class in the middle of the year when everybody has already made friends with everybody else. But it's close.

When I arrived, the class hardly noticed me standing there in a corner wearing my "new-boy" grin. They were all excited because they had to do a show the very next evening for the Parents' Club. It was a play about Robin Hood that they had written themselves. It was really good. But I felt lonely watching them practice. I wanted to be part of it. So I got this terrific idea.

"Mrs. Clark!" I yelled. "What this play needs is music!"

The class looked at Mrs. Clark with that expression kids have when a new boy says something, as if he were speaking Eskimo.

"What, Rick?" Mrs. Clark called, trying to keep the curtains from knocking over Sherwood Forest.

"Music," I repeated. "You know, something graceful when Robin Hood meets Maid Marian, something exciting when the Sheriff chases Robin, something merry when the Merry Men have their feast.''

"Do you play an instrument?" Mrs. Clark asked.

"No," I admitted. I caught a glimpse of one girl giggling.

"Music would be nice, Rick," Mrs. Clark said, in that kindly way teachers talk to the new pupil when they know he's trying hard. "But if you don't play an instrument . . . "

"The tape recorder!" I cried.

"You play the tape recorder?" Mrs. Clark wondered.

"I could record music for each scene on a tape recorder. Then all I'd have to do is turn the recorder on and off at the right times."

"That will be a nice challenge for you, Rick," Mrs. Clark said, with the smile of a teacher who has just discovered the new boy may turn out all right. "There are the tape recorder and my records. And here's a copy of the play to follow. Good luck!"

I thanked her and she turned away to get the actors started again. Actually, things weren't going as I'd hoped. Instead of being with the rest of the class, I was alone in a corner again.

"Never mind," I told myself. "Just do the best job ever done by a boy and a tape recorder and you'll have more friends than you know what to do with."

What a challenge it turned out to be! I went through all Mrs. Clark's records, trying to match music to the different moods of the play. I worked every free minute I had. Then I took the tape recorder home. I worked with my parents' records, too.

Finally, I had it. It was the best arrangement of music ever tape-recorded for a play about Robin Hood and his Merry Men by any fifth-grade pupil. My first choice was a trumpet call as the curtain opened. Then came merry music for the Merry Men, angry music for the Sheriff, brave music for Robin, graceful music for Marian, and wild music for the big chase through the forest. I could hardly wait to get to school the next morning.

"Here's our music man," announced Mrs. Clark, the minute I arrived.

"Can I play it for the class now?" I asked.

"I'm afraid not," Mrs. Clark answered. "We're going to practice this morning, but so many teachers have asked if their classes could see the play. I told them we'd make our last practice time a regular show for the school."

In no time, we were behind the closed curtain and other classes were marching into the auditorium. Mrs. Clark placed me and my tape recorder to one side of the stage where the audience couldn't see us.

Suddenly the curtain opened. Mrs. Clark gave me a signal, and I pushed the button and the trumpet call began. Then, the thought struck me: I'd never practiced with the class, not even once! No sooner had the trumpet call ended then I knew how much I'd missed. The other kids had never learned to wait for the music. Before I knew it, the Merry Men were off and I caught a glimpse of Maid

Marian and Robin talking to the angry music. The harder I tried to catch up or go back, the worse things got. The Sheriff ended up yelling at Robin to Marian's graceful music. Robin declared his love for Marian during my choice for the chase music through the woods. It was crazy!

In fifteen minutes it was over, but the audience clapped and roared for another five. When the auditorium lights came on, the actors looked at Mrs. Clark with expressions that said, "Will you kill that new boy or should we?"

"Rick," Mrs. Clark gasped, "you've turned our play into a . . . a joke!"

I grinned nervously. "The audience thought it was terrific," I offered.

Mrs. Clark's mouth fell open and she looked surprised. "They did!" she exclaimed. She started laughing, and the class began laughing with her and cheering and patting me on the back.

I had plenty of friends after that, but just then I was shaking too hard to care. It's not the worst thing in the world trying to win over a whole fifth grade at once and doing it completely backwards. But it's close.

It's Not the Worst Thing in the World

COMPREHENSION CHECK

Choose the best answer.

1. Rick was
   _____ a. lost.
   _____ b. the new boy in class.
   _____ c. not very friendly.
   _____ d. not going to school.

2. The class was excited because
   _____ a. there was a bad storm.
   _____ b. there was a fire.
   _____ c. they had to produce a play.
   _____ d. they were late.

3. The play was about
   _____ a. a famous detective.
   _____ b. a fourth-grade class.
   _____ c. children in another country.
   _____ d. Robin Hood.

4. Mrs. Clark was
   _____ a. Rick's new teacher.
   _____ b. Rick's mother.
   _____ c. a character in the play.
   _____ d. the principal.

5. Rick's terrific idea
   _____ a. was to write a new play.
   _____ b. made Mrs. Clark angry.
   _____ c. worked just as he thought it would.
   _____ d. was to tape-record music for the play.

6. The audience
   _____ a. thought the play was terrible.
   _____ b. thought the play was terrific.
   _____ c. did not want to see the play.
   _____ d. was late for the play.

7. When the play was over,
   _____ a. Rick had plenty of friends.
   _____ b. Rick ran home crying.
   _____ c. the audience was angry.
   _____ d. Mrs. Clark would not speak to Rick.

8. One thing that kept Rick's spirit up was
   _____ a. not caring about making new friends.
   _____ b. a sense of humor about being "new."
   _____ c. hoping that the play would be bad.
   _____ d. not having a part in the play.

9. Another name for this story could be
   _____ a. "Robin Hood."
   _____ b. "Mrs. Clark's Play."
   _____ c. "How to Perform a Play."
   _____ d. "The New Boy's Challenge."

10. This story is mainly about
    _____ a. choosing a play.
    _____ b. going to school.
    _____ c. making friends in a new school.
    _____ d. children writing a play.

Check your answers with the key on page 53.

Idea starter: Why are "terrific ideas" not always successful?

It's Not the Worst Thing in the World

VOCABULARY CHECK

challenge	choice	expression	glimpse	graceful	terrific

I.   Write the correct key word from the box above in each of the following blanks.

1.   You are going to pitch in the big game. What a _____ !

2.   You get an A in your spelling test. Wow! That's _____ !

3.   You look at your Mom and you know she's proud of you. You can tell

by her _____ .

4.   Your friends want you to play but you have chores to do. You must make a _____ .

5.   You feel silly because you fell on your face at the skating party. You wanted to

appear _____ .

6.   There goes your best friend riding by on that bus! You just caught a _____ of her.

II.   Underline the key word that belongs in each sentence.

1.   Diving is a very **graceful glimpse** sport.

2.   Each student may take the seat of his or her **expression choice** .

3.   A hard job is more pleasant if you accept it as a **challenge graceful** .

4.   Did you get a **glimpse terrific** of the new girl in school?

5.   Why does she have such a disappointed **graceful expression** ?

6.   I think our new teacher is **challenge terrific** .

Check your answers with the key on page 58.

This page may be reproduced for classroom use.

From Latvia, for Christmas

Learn the Key Words

blur   (blėr)   something difficult to see because it is dim or unclear
Everything becomes a <u>blur</u> when I take off my glasses.

chaos   (kā′ os)   a situation in which everything is wildly confused
The moment the winning point was made, <u>chaos</u> broke out among the fans.

meek   (mēk)   humble; shy
Although he knew the answer, he was too <u>meek</u> to say it.

nudge   (nuj)   a soft push
Janet's <u>nudge</u> reminded me to cross the street.

pronunciation   (prə nun sē ā′ shən)   the way in which words are spoken, or pronounced
I can tell by your <u>pronunciation</u> that you are from New York.

rehearse   (ri hėrs′)   to practice again and again
We'll <u>rehearse</u> our play every day after school.

Preview:

1. Read the title.
2. Look at the picture.
3. Read the first paragraph of the story.
4. Then answer the following question.

You learned from your preview that
_____ a. a house had been damaged by a hurricane.
_____ b. Mom and Dad like to read or watch TV.
_____ c. Christmas Eve was a peaceful time.
_____ d. many guests were always present on Christmas.

Turn to the Comprehension Check on page 44 for the right answer.

Now read the story.
Read to find out how Aunt Sophie changed one family's holidays.

From Latvia, for Christmas

Aunt Sophie's old-fashioned customs traveled with her.

A place you will read about:	Latvia	(lat′ vē ə)	a land in northern Europe

All year, the chaos of a hurricane fills our house. Mom, Dad, Ricky, and I are always dashing to work, or to school, or to meetings. But Christmas Eve and Christmas Day the chaos lessens because the four of us are alone together. That is why I was upset when it seemed that our Christmas holidays might be changed by the visit of Aunt Sophie, Dad's sister from Latvia.

A week before Christmas she stood in our living room, gray-haired, meek, and silent. Dad was working late at the post office. All through dinner, Mom smiled and tried to make conversation while Aunt Sophie nodded or mumbled and stared at her plate. She didn't eat a bite, not even of Mom's extra-special chocolate cake for extra-special occasions. As I finished my last crumb, I felt Ricky nudge me under the table. Together we escaped into the kitchen to do the dishes, in no hurry to get back to Aunt Sophie.

After a while, Mom came after us. "Aunt Sophie has traveled a long way. You must be especially nice to her," she said.

"She's not especially nice to us," Ricky said.

"She hasn't smiled once since she arrived," I added.

"She's frightened, Andrea," Mom said. "This is her first trip outside Latvia. Coming here wasn't easy for her. A couple of good-night kisses might help."

Her nudge sent Ricky and me shuffling out of the kitchen and over to Aunt Sophie. "Good night," we muttered, each brushing a quick kiss across her wrinkled forehead.

"Yes, yes, good night," she whispered, patting our arms as if making sure we were real.

Ricky and I raced upstairs.

Soon Dad came home. "Sophie! Oh, Sophie!" he cried.

Ricky and I dashed to the stairs and peered down to find Dad and Aunt Sophie clinging to each other and crying.

"Edmund, my Edmund, it has been twenty years!"

It was one gloomy meeting.

Suddenly, Dad smiled. "All day I've been remembering Christmas in Latvia: the snow, the special bread, and Christmas Man. How I would hide when he burst into our house! And then, how we would sing and dance for him!"

"Dad and Aunt Sophie dancing?" Ricky yelped, giving us away.

"Come down, you two," Dad called. "Now that Aunt Sophie is here, let's have an old-fashioned Latvian Christmas."

But I wanted my kind of Christmas, with just my own family.

Dad went on excitedly. "You kids better prepare something for Christmas Man and rehearse it until it's good. If you don't entertain him properly on Christmas Eve, you'll get brushwood switches instead of toys."

"I'll play my guitar," Ricky offered. "Could you teach me Latvian songs, Aunt Sophie?"

"Of course," Aunt Sophie beamed, meek no longer.

From then on, she and Ricky were always together, humming and plucking out Latvian melodies. That left me hours to wander around the house alone, feeling disappointed and sorry for myself. Then one morning, Mom asked what I would perform for Christmas Man.

"Oh, that's for little kids like Ricky," I muttered.

"No," answered Mom, "it's for big kids like Daddy. A Latvian Christmas would be the best present we could give him."

I wasn't happy about it, but I knew she was right. So I asked Ricky and Aunt Sophie if I could rehearse with them. In her funny Latvian-style pronunciation, Aunt Sophie welcomed me. Then the hours flew by in a busy blur as she kept us singing, dancing, and making Latvian tree decorations. Finally, we baked sweet-sour bread, and it was Christmas Eve.

Dad worked late, but we decorated the tree and loaded the table with homemade treats. Snow started to fall, and our house looked, smelled, and felt like an old-fashioned Latvian home.

Dad's car pulled up and we stopped talking while he opened the front door. His face glowed and kept on glowing as we ate, read the Christmas story aloud, and sang carols.

"What a beautiful Christmas," Aunt Sophie sighed.

"Let's do it every year," Ricky said. "Stay with us, Aunt Sophie."

Aunt Sophie shook her head and answered, "Latvia is my home. All my family and friends are there, except for you."

For a moment, Aunt Sophie looked so sad I knew she was missing being in Latvia. Suddenly, I realized how much she had given up to visit us. And I'd been thinking only of what I'd given up! I jumped up to hug her, and the room became a blur before my tear-filled eyes.

"I wish they all could have come here, Aunt Sophie," I said. And I meant it.

Just then, Christmas Man, wearing boots, a long coat, and a high fur hat, threw open the door. With his face mysteriously hidden behind a dark beard he was terrifying.

"Are there any lazy children here for me to spank?" he roared, imitating Aunt Sophie's Latvian pronunciation.

"No!" laughed Aunt Sophie.

"Prove it!" insisted Christmas Man.

Ricky grabbed his guitar and we sang and danced as Aunt Sophie had taught us. Dad clapped his hands joyfully. Then everyone danced along, even Christmas Man (who turned out to be Mom's brother, Uncle Henry).

We twirled and sang until we were exhausted.

Finally, we opened our gifts. I've forgotten exactly what I got that year, except for the best present of all: Aunt Sophie and our old-fashioned Latvian Christmas.

From Latvia, for Christmas

COMPREHENSION CHECK

Choose the best answer.

1. Most of the year, Andrea's house was
   ____ a. quiet and dull.
   ____ b. filled with chaos.
   ____ c. empty.
   ____ d. a gloomy place.

2. On Christmas day, Andrea's family liked
   ____ a. to take time to be with each other.
   ____ b. to go shopping.
   ____ c. to go to work.
   ____ d. to spend time away from each other.

3. When Aunt Sophie first arrived, she was
   ____ a. cold and hungry.
   ____ b. excited and happy.
   ____ c. meek and quiet.
   ____ d. very friendly.

4. Aunt Sophie taught Ricky and Andrea
   ____ a. Latvian songs and dances.
   ____ b. how to read.
   ____ c. Christmas carols from England.
   ____ d. card games.

5. On Christmas Eve, the children had to entertain
   ____ a. their neighbors.
   ____ b. each other.
   ____ c. a group of strangers.
   ____ d. Christmas Man.

6. When he burst into the house, Christmas Man was
   ____ a. quiet.
   ____ b. friendly.
   ____ c. terrifying.
   ____ d. nervous.

7. Andrea's favorite present that Christmas was
   ____ a. the snow and the homemade treats.
   ____ b. Aunt Sophie and the old-fashioned Latvian Christmas.
   ____ c. Mom's extra-special chocolate cake.
   ____ d. the one Christmas Man gave her.

8. Latvian Christmas customs
   ____ a. are exactly like American customs.
   ____ b. are completely different from American customs.
   ____ c. are like ours, but do not include Christmas trees.
   ____ d. are like ours, but include visits from Christmas Man.

9. Another name for this story could be
   ____ a. "Andrea Visits Latvia."
   ____ b. "Ricky's Guitar."
   ____ c. "Christmas Strangers, Christmas Friends."
   ____ d. "Latvian Songs and Dances."

10. This story is mainly about
    ____ a. a girl who learns to love her aunt from Latvia.
    ____ b. Christmas customs all over the world.
    ____ c. a brother and a sister who don't get along.
    ____ d. a girl who doesn't like her Christmas presents.

Check your answers with the key on page 53.

Idea starter: Why did Andrea think that Aunt Sophie and the old-fashioned Christmas was the best present?

From Latvia, for Christmas

VOCABULARY CHECK

| blur | chaos | meek | nudge | pronunciation | rehearse |

I.   Unscramble your key words and use them to complete the sentences.

1.   runiacnotipno   Careful _____ makes your speech easier to understand.

2.   ekme   She wanted more ice cream, but she was too _____ to ask for it.

3.   saeerhre   We'll _____ this song until we can do it without any mistakes.

4.   rlbu   Raindrops on the window made everything outside a _____ .

5.   gdune   He will wake up if you _____ him.

6.   asohc   Every time the teacher leaves that class alone, there is _____ .

II.   Draw a line connecting each key word with the words that belong with it.

blur   wild confusion

chaos   quiet; shy; humble

meek   dim; unclear

nudge   practice; repeat

pronunciation   push; poke; shove

rehearse   speech; sound

Check your answers with the key on page 59.

The Chimp Who "Talks" to People

Learn the Key Words

achievement   (ə chēv′ mənt)   something done well
Learning to ski was an <u>achievement</u> for a boy with one leg.

automatic   (ô tə mat′ ik)
1. moving by itself
   An <u>automatic</u> light goes on when seat belts aren't fastened.
2. done without thought

indignant   (in dig′ nənt)   angry about some unfair or unjust treatment
Susie broke a glass, and Robbie became <u>indignant</u> when Mom blamed him.

remarkable   (ri mär′ kə bəl)   unusual; not ordinary
It was <u>remarkable</u> that no one was hurt in the fire.

situation   (sich ü ā′ shən)
1. a personal condition; a state of affairs
   Getting caught in a lie was a difficult <u>situation</u> for Sam to handle.
2. a job

symbol   (sim′ bəl)   a sign or letter that stands for something else
Instead of writing out the word ''number,'' you can use the <u>symbol</u> #.

Preview:
1. Read the title.
2. Look at the picture.
3. Read the first paragraph of the story.
4. Then answer the following question.

You learned from your preview that
_____ a. a computer was designed by a chimp.
_____ b. a chimp has taught a computer to hum.
_____ c. a chimp has been used in an experiment.
_____ d. all animals can ''talk'' and be understood.

Turn to the Comprehension Check on page 49 for the right answer.

Now read the story.
Read to find out why Lana has been trained by scientists.

The Chimp Who "Talks" to People

Lana's knowledge of symbols brings her many rewards.

Things you will read about:		
chimp	(chimp)	a short form of *chimpanzee*
computer	(kəm pyü′ tər)	a machine that solves problems and performs many tasks at high speed
M&M's	(em and emz′)	the name of a special candy

Picture a room with glass walls. On one wall, there is a keyboard with colored push buttons. Above it is a viewing screen. Hundreds of wires lead from the keyboard into a humming computer. What you're looking at is a room designed especially for an experiment with a young chimp. This has been a remarkable experiment, for it has taught people that they are not the only creatures who can "talk" and have their language understood.

It all began in 1972. Scientist Timothy Gill brought a two-year-old chimp named Lana into the glass room. This room would be her home for years to come.

Tim began by showing Lana how the colored buttons on the keyboard lit up when he pushed them. Each button had a symbol on it—a circle or square or wavy line or several of them together. Each symbol was on a different colored background for different kinds of words. Red was used for food and drink words. Purple was used for people words. And blue was used for action words.

Lana copied Tim and started pushing the buttons herself. She got to know the water symbol quickly, since a drink came down into a cup each time she pushed it. But she got to know the "M&M" symbol even more quickly, for whenever she pushed it, her favorite candy dropped out of the machine.

Then the scientists adjusted the machine. Now, the machine would give Lana what she wanted only when she pushed the "please" button before asking and the "period" button after asking. They weren't trying to teach her to be polite. The "please" button told the computer that Lana was about to ask for something. And the "period" button let it know that she was finished. It could now give her what she asked for. In a few days, Lana learned to punch out "Please M&M." and get her M&M's.

As new symbols were added to Lana's keyboard, she began punching out real sentences. "Please M&M." became "Please machine give me Lana M&M." But the scientists had to make sure that Lana was really learning her new symbols. They had to make sure that she wasn't just remembering their positions on the keyboard. So, to be sure, they changed these positions on the keyboard every day.

As Lana learned to push each button, she also learned to look up at the screen. There, she "read" the symbols as they appeared in a row from left to right as words in a sentence. This was not something she had been taught. It was something she had begun doing herself to check what she had punched. When Lana pushed the wrong button and saw her mistake flash on the screen, she would push the "period" button. She had learned without help that this "period" button was a kind of automatic eraser. It cleared the screen and let her try again. The scientists admit that they didn't intend to use the "period" button as an automatic eraser. But Lana had taught them a new use for it.

This remarkable chimp even taught herself to describe something when she didn't have a symbol for it. One day, Tim came into the laboratory with an orange. Lana wanted it. How could she handle this situation? There was no symbol for the fruit "orange" on her keyboard. But there was one for "apple" and one for the color "orange." So Lana handled the situation by punching out: "Please Tim give apple which is orange-color."

Soon, Lana was demanding new symbols for things she saw and wanted. One morning, Tim walked in with a box of candy. Lana wanted it, but she had no symbol for "box." So she tried asking Tim to give her the "bowl" or the "can"—two symbols she did have. Tim refused. But Lana didn't give up.

She punched out: "Please Tim give Lana name of this."

Tim punched out on his own keyboard: "Box name of this." And Lana immediately punched back: "Please Tim give Lana this box."

Usually Lana enjoyed showing off an achievement to guests. But during one visit, while she was at her keyboard punching out her sentence, Tim tricked her. He used his own keyboard to slip a wrong word into her sentence. Lana hit the "period" button to clear the screen; then she began again. But again, Tim slipped in a wrong word. Lana became indignant, but she tried once more. And once more, Tim slipped in a wrong word. Lana then decided that the guests were to blame for the mistake. More indignant than ever, she looked at the visitors and punched out on her keyboard: "Please move outside of the room." This remarkable chimp had actually chased her guests out of the room!

What is the purpose behind all these experiments? Scientists believe that by studying Lana's achievements they can help children who cannot speak. How remarkable an achievement it will be for the children of that silent world to be able to push buttons and "talk" with symbols to the noisy world around them!

The Chimp Who "Talks" to People

COMPREHENSION CHECK

Choose the best answer.

1. Lana's room has glass walls because
   _____ a. chimps don't like solid ones.
   _____ b. chimps like to feel as if they're outdoors.
   _____ c. the scientists have to be able to watch her.
   _____ d. she asked for them on the keyboard.

2. The symbols on the keyboard were
   _____ a. letters of the alphabet.
   _____ b. pictures of everyday objects.
   _____ c. words Lana had to read.
   _____ d. circles, squares, and lines.

3. To make sure Lana wasn't remembering the symbols by their positions on the keyboard, the scientists
   _____ a. covered Lana's eyes with a cloth.
   _____ b. changed these positions daily.
   _____ c. added new words every day.
   _____ d. took away the keyboard once a week.

4. Lana discovered that the "period" button
   _____ a. was an automatic eraser.
   _____ b. always gave her M&M's.
   _____ c. changed the symbols on the screen.
   _____ d. told her she had made a mistake.

5. Lana handled the situation of the orange by
   _____ a. deciding she didn't want it.
   _____ b. throwing it at the visitors.
   _____ c. grabbing it from Tim's hand.
   _____ d. describing it as an orange-colored apple.

6. Lana became indignant when
   _____ a. Tim wouldn't add new symbols to her keyboard.
   _____ b. the guests took away her M&M's.
   _____ c. Tim slipped a wrong word in her sentence.
   _____ d. Tim wouldn't give her the box of candy.

7. Lana can be called a remarkable chimp because
   _____ a. most chimps can't live in a laboratory.
   _____ b. she showed how intelligent chimps really are.
   _____ c. she liked to eat "people food."
   _____ d. she taught other chimps to work the keyboard.

8. Scientists are studying Lana's achievement in order
   _____ a. to help children who cannot speak.
   _____ b. to make chimps smarter.
   _____ c. to see if fruit is healthy for chimps.
   _____ d. to decide if chimps can live inside glass walls.

9. Another name for this story could be
   _____ a. "A Chimp's Life in the Jungle."
   _____ b. "Trapped in a Laboratory."
   _____ c. "Chimps Have No Intelligence."
   _____ d. "Lana Learns a Language."

10. This story is mainly about
    _____ a. a friendship between a scientist and a chimp.
    _____ b. teaching a chimp to recognize colors.
    _____ c. a chimp who learned to talk to people with symbols.
    _____ d. training a chimp to do tricks in a laboratory.

Check your answers with the key on page 53.

Idea starter: What are some other experiments in which animals have been used?

The Chimp Who "Talks" to People

VOCABULARY CHECK

achievement	automatic	indignant	remarkable	situation	symbol

I. *Your six key words are scrambled. Set them straight and use them to fill in the blanks.*

1. nantgidin   Don became _____ when he lost the race.

2. inousatit   Moving to a different city was a new _____ for Ellen.

3. blosmy   On a map, a star is used as a _____ for a capital city.

4. blamereark   Andy's _____ pictures of the fire were printed in the newspaper.

5. ucaitotma   The _____ controls turn on the heat when the weather is cold.

6. theenivacem   For a blind person to become a lawyer is a great _____ .

II. *Put an X next to the sentence in which the underlined key word is used correctly.*

1. _____ a. The discovery of a vaccination against polio was Dr. Salk's brilliant <u>achievement</u>.
   _____ b. Losing the battle was an amazing <u>achievement</u>.

2. _____ a. The <u>automatic</u> timer shuts off the oven.
   _____ b. An <u>automatic</u> elevator needs someone to run it.

3. _____ a. A raise in salary made Jeff <u>indignant</u>.
   _____ b. Seeing her garbage pails turned over made Mrs. Lee <u>indignant</u>.

4. _____ a. It was <u>remarkable</u> to see snow in Alaska.
   _____ b. With our star batter hurt, it was <u>remarkable</u> that we won the game.

5. _____ a. Her father's death was a difficult <u>situation</u> for Eve to handle.
   _____ b. Carla went to the museum to see a <u>situation</u> of new paintings.

6. _____ a. Be sure to write the dollar <u>symbol</u> in your answer.
   _____ b. Billy hid his <u>symbol</u> under his pillow.

Check your answers with the key on page 59.

This page may be reproduced for classroom use

KEY WORDS
Lessons E-21—E-30

E-21

appeal
athletic
benefit
celebration
horror
memory

E-22

astonishment
bluff
crime
dusk
ransom
sip

E-23

attach
captive
distress
patience
terrify
thus

E-24

breed
brilliant
glorious
limit
total
twig

E-25

aware
cautious
inhabitant
ridiculous
theory
visible

E-26

fury
marvel
miracle
numb
rely
strife

KEY WORDS
Lessons E-21—E-30

E-27

admiration
chemistry
disguise
fabulous
laboratory
sergeant

E-28

challenge
choice
expression
glimpse
graceful
terrific

E-29

blur
chaos
meek
nudge
pronunciation
rehearse

E-30

achievement
automatic
indignant
remarkable
situation
symbol

COMPREHENSION CHECK ANSWER KEY
Lessons E-21—E-30

LESSON NUMBER	QUESTION NUMBER										PAGE NUMBER
	1	2	3	4	5	6	7	8	9	10	
E-21	b	a	c	c	ⓓ	b	c	d	△d	[b]	4
E-22	c	b	a	c	c	d	ⓓ	b	△c	[d]	9
E-23	b	d	d	c	c	d	b	ⓐ	△d	[a]	14
E-24	b	b	a	d	c	b	a	ⓓ	△c	[a]	19
E-25	c	c	c	d	d	c	a	ⓓ	△b	[a]	24
E-26	a	c	b	c	a	b	d	ⓐ	△c	[b]	29
E-27	d	b	c	c	a	d	b	ⓒ	△c	[d]	34
E-28	b	c	d	a	d	b	a	ⓑ	△d	[c]	39
E-29	b	a	c	a	d	c	b	ⓓ	△c	[a]	44
E-30	ⓒ	d	b	a	d	c	ⓑ	a	△d	[c]	49

Code: ◯ = Inference

△ = Another Name for the Selection

☐ = Main Idea

NOTES

VOCABULARY CHECK ANSWER KEY
Lessons E-21—E-30

E-21   *WE REMEMBER ROBERTO*   5

I.
1. athletic
2. horror
3. benefit
4. memory
5. celebration
6. appeal

II.
1. b
2. c
3. d
4. a
5. b
6. a

E-22   *THE KIDNAPPING OF BINKY MARLOWE*   10

I.
1. sip
2. bluff
3. dusk
4. astonishment
5. crime
6. ransom

II.
1. ~~bluff~~ sip
2. ~~astonishment~~ crime
3. dusk ~~ransom~~
4. bluff ~~crime~~
5. ~~dusk~~ ransom
6. astonishment ~~sip~~

VOCABULARY CHECK ANSWER KEY
Lessons E-21—E-30

E-23 *THE CLEANERS*   15

I.   1. | A | T | T | A | C | H |
     2. | T | H | U | S |
     3. | D | I | S | T | R | E | S | S |
     4. | T | E | R | R | I | F | Y |
     5. | P | A | T | I | E | N | C | E |
     6. | C | A | P | T | I | V | E |

II. 1. attach
       2. thus
       3. distress
       4. terrify
       5. patience
       6. captive

E-24 *THE PASSENGER PIGEON*   20

I.   1. limit
       2. brilliant *or* glorious
       3. total
       4. breed
       5. brilliant *or* glorious
       6. twig

II.

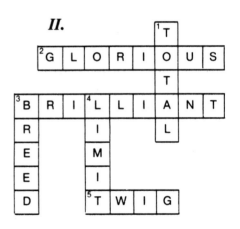

VOCABULARY CHECK ANSWER KEY
Lessons E-21—E-30

E-25 **THE LOCH NESS MONSTER**   25

I. 1. visible   *II.* 1. b
      2. inhabitant   2. a
      3. theory   3. b
      4. aware   4. a
      5. cautious   5. b
      6. ridiculous   6. b

E-26 **"TELL US WHY, PETER"**   30

I. 1. strife   *II.* 1. numb
      2. marvel   2. fury
      3. fury   3. rely
      4. rely   4. strife
      5. miracle   5. marvel
      6. numb   6. miracle

VOCABULARY CHECK ANSWER KEY
Lessons E-21—E-30

I.
1. fabulous
2. sergeant
3. admiration
4. laboratory
5. disguise
6. chemistry

II.
1. admiration ~~fabulous~~
2. ~~laboratory~~ sergeant
3. ~~chemistry~~ fabulous
4. ~~admiration~~ laboratory
5. disguise ~~sergeant~~
6. chemistry ~~disguise~~

I.
1. challenge
2. terrific
3. expression
4. choice
5. graceful
6. glimpse

II.
1. graceful
2. choice
3. challenge
4. glimpse
5. expression
6. terrific

VOCABULARY CHECK ANSWER KEY
Lessons E-21—E-30

E-29 *FROM LATVIA, FOR CHRISTMAS*   45

    I. 1. pronunciation
        2. meek
        3. rehearse
        4. blur
        5. nudge
        6. chaos

II. 1.
blur — dim; unclear
chaos — wild confusion
meek — quiet; shy; humble
nudge — push; poke; shove
pronunciation — speech; sound
rehearse — practice; repeat

E-30 *THE CHIMP WHO "TALKS" TO PEOPLE*   50

    I. 1. indignant
        2. situation
        3. symbol
        4. remarkable
        5. automatic
        6. achievement

    II. 1. a
         2. a
         3. b
         4. b
         5. a
         6. a

NOTES